SCOTT FORESMAN

READING STREET

*KINDERGARTEN*

COMMON CORE ©

# Program Authors

Peter Afflerbach

Camille Blachowicz

Candy Dawson Boyd

Elena Izquierdo

Connie Juel

Edward Kame'enui

Donald Leu

Jeanne R. Paratore

P. David Pearson

Sam Sebesta

Deborah Simmons

Susan Watts Taffe

Alfred Tatum

Sharon Vaughn

Karen Kring Wixson

**Glenview, Illinois**

**Boston, Massachusetts**

**Chandler, Arizona**

**Upper Saddle River, New Jersey**

ALWAYS LEARNING

PEARSON

*We dedicate Reading Street to*
*Peter Jovanovich.*

*His wisdom, courage,*
*and passion for education*
*are an inspiration to us all.*

Accelerated Reader®

Acknowledgments appear on page 144, which constitutes an extension of this copyright page.

ISBN-13: 978-0-328-72442-0
ISBN-10:    0-328-72442-4
2 3 4 5 6 7 8 9 10 V042 16 15 14 13 12

**Reading**
STREET

Dear Reader,

Just think about how much you've learned on Reading Street this year! The year is almost over, but we have one last trip. You can use all of the skills and ideas you've learned to help you enjoy it.

This trip will take us to places where animals are building homes and boats, and people are building houses and schools. Keep your thinking caps on. We still have a lot to learn.

AlphaBuddy says, "It's been great working and playing with you. Keep on reading!"

Sincerely,
The Authors

## Unit 6 Contents

**Putting It Together**

**What are different ways of building?**

### Week 1

Let's Listen for Vowel Sounds . . . . . . . . . . . . . . . . . **12**

Comprehension: Compare and Contrast . . . . . . . . . **14**

Phonics and High-Frequency Words . . . . . . . . . . . . **16**

I Can Read! Decodable Reader 31

If Kip Can . . . . . . . . . . . . . . . . . . . . . . . . **18**

Informational Fiction • Social Studies
**Building with Dad** by Carol Nevius
Retell/Think, Talk, and Write . . . . . . . . . . . . . . . **26**

Big Book

Let's Learn It! . . . . . . . . . . . . . . . . . . . . . . . . . . . **28**

Let's Practice It! Expository Text . . . . . . . . . . . . . **30**

## Week 2

Let's Listen for Vowel Sounds . . . . . . . . . . . . . . . . 32

Comprehension: Literary Elements . . . . . . . . . . . 34

Phonics and High-Frequency Words . . . . . . . . . . 36

**I Can Read!** Decodable Reader 32

Will Cass Come? . . . . . . . . . . . . . . . . . . . . . . . 38

Trade Book

**Animal Fantasy • Science**

## Old MacDonald Had a Woodshop
by Lisa Shulman

Retell/Think, Talk, and Write . . . . . . . . . . . . . . . 46

Let's Learn It! . . . . . . . . . . . . . . . . . . . . . . . . . . 48

Let's Practice It! Lullaby . . . . . . . . . . . . . . . . . . . 50

# Unit 6 Contents

## Week 3

Let's Listen for Vowel Sounds . . . . . . . . . . . . . . . . 52

Comprehension: Main Idea . . . . . . . . . . . . . . 54

Phonics and High-Frequency Words . . . . . . . . . . 56

I Can Read! Decodable Reader 33

The Red Egg . . . . . . . . . . . . . . . . . . . . . . . . . 58

**Expository Nonfiction • Science**

**Building Beavers** by Kathleen Martin-James

Retell/Think, Talk, and Write . . . . . . . . . . . . . . 66

Big Book

Let's Learn It! . . . . . . . . . . . . . . . . . . . . . . . . 68

Let's Practice It! Fable . . . . . . . . . . . . . . . . . . 70

## Week 4

Let's Listen for Vowel Sounds . . . . . . . . . . . . . . . . 72

Comprehension: Literary Elements . . . . . . . . . . . . 74

Phonics and High-Frequency Words . . . . . . . . . . 76

I Can Read! Decodable Reader 34

Fun with Spot . . . . . . . . . . . . . . . . . . . . . . . . 78

**Animal Fantasy • Social Studies**

**Alistair and Kip's Great Adventure!**
by John Segal

Retell/Think, Talk, and Write . . . . . . . . . . . . . . 86

Trade Book

Let's Learn It! . . . . . . . . . . . . . . . . . . . . . . . . 88

Let's Practice It! Signs . . . . . . . . . . . . . . . . . . 90

## Week 5

Let's Listen for Consonant and Vowel Sounds . . ◆ 92

Comprehension: Literary Elements . . . . . . . . . . ◆ 94

Phonics and High-Frequency Words . . . . . . . . . ◆ 96

I Can Read! Decodable Reader 35

   Fun in the Sun . . . . . . . . . . . . . . . . . . . . . . ◆ 98

Big Book

**Informational Fiction • Social Studies**
## The House That Tony Lives In
by Anthony Lorenz

**Retell/Think, Talk, and Write** . . . . . . . . . . . . . . ◆ 106

Let's Learn It! . . . . . . . . . . . . . . . . . . . . . . . . . . ◆ 108

Let's Practice It! Folk Tale . . . . . . . . . . . . . . . . ◆ 110

## Week 6

Let's Listen for Blends . . . . . . . . . . . . . . . . . . . . ★ 112

Comprehension: Draw Conclusions . . . . . . . . . . ★ 114

Phonics and High-Frequency Words . . . . . . . . . . ★ 116

I Can Read! Decodable Reader 36

   The Box . . . . . . . . . . . . . . . . . . . . . . . . . . . . ★ 118

Trade Book

**Expository Nonfiction • Science**
## Ants and Their Nests by Linda Tagliaferro

**Retell/Think, Talk, and Write** . . . . . . . . . . . . . ★ 126

Let's Learn It! . . . . . . . . . . . . . . . . . . . . . . . . . . ★ 128

Let's Practice It! Poetry . . . . . . . . . . . . . . . . . . ★ 130

**Don Leu**
**The Internet Guy**

Right before our eyes, the nature of reading and learning is changing. The Internet and other technologies create new opportunities, new solutions, and new literacies. New reading comprehension skills are required online. They are increasingly important to our students and our society.

Those of us on the Reading Street team are here to help you on this new, and very exciting, journey.

## See It!

- Big Question Video

- Concept Talk Video

- Envision It! Animations

- eReaders

## Hear It!

- *Sing with Me* **Animations**

- eSelections

Adam and Kim **play at the beach.**

- Grammar Jammer

Concept Talk Video

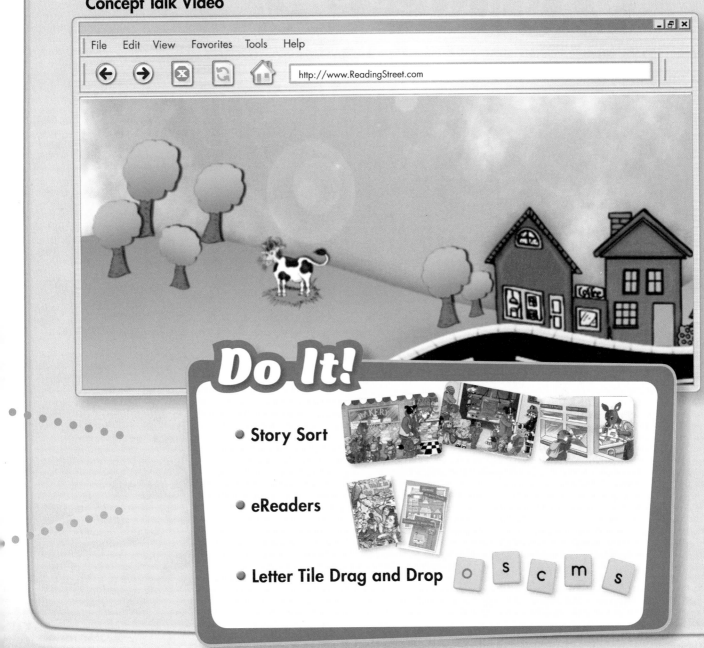

| File | Edit | View | Favorites | Tools | Help |

http://www.ReadingStreet.com

## Do It!

- Story Sort

- eReaders

- Letter Tile Drag and Drop   o   s   c   m   s

# Putting It Together

## What are different ways of building?

**Common Core State Standards**
**Foundational Skills 2.d.** Isolate and pronounce the initial, medial vowel, and final sounds (phonemes) in three-phoneme (consonant-vowel-consonant, or CVC) words. **Also Foundational Skills 2.e.**

# Let's Listen for

**Read Together**

## Vowel Sounds

● Point to the apple. Say the word. Say the beginning sound.

■ Point to the igloo. Say the word. Say the beginning sound.

▲ Find three things that begin with /a/, like *apple*. Find three things that begin with /i/, like *igloo*.

★ Point to these pictures and say the words: *ax, apple, animal*. Do they begin the same? What about *igloo, alligator, umbrella?*

♥ Point to a hat. What sounds do you hear in *hat?* Separate the sounds with me: /h/ /a/ /t/.

**READING STREET ONLINE**
**BIG QUESTION VIDEO**
www.ReadingStreet.com

Comprehension

# Envision It!

## Compare and Contrast

**READING STREET ONLINE**
**ENVISION IT! ANIMATIONS**
www.ReadingStreet.com

14

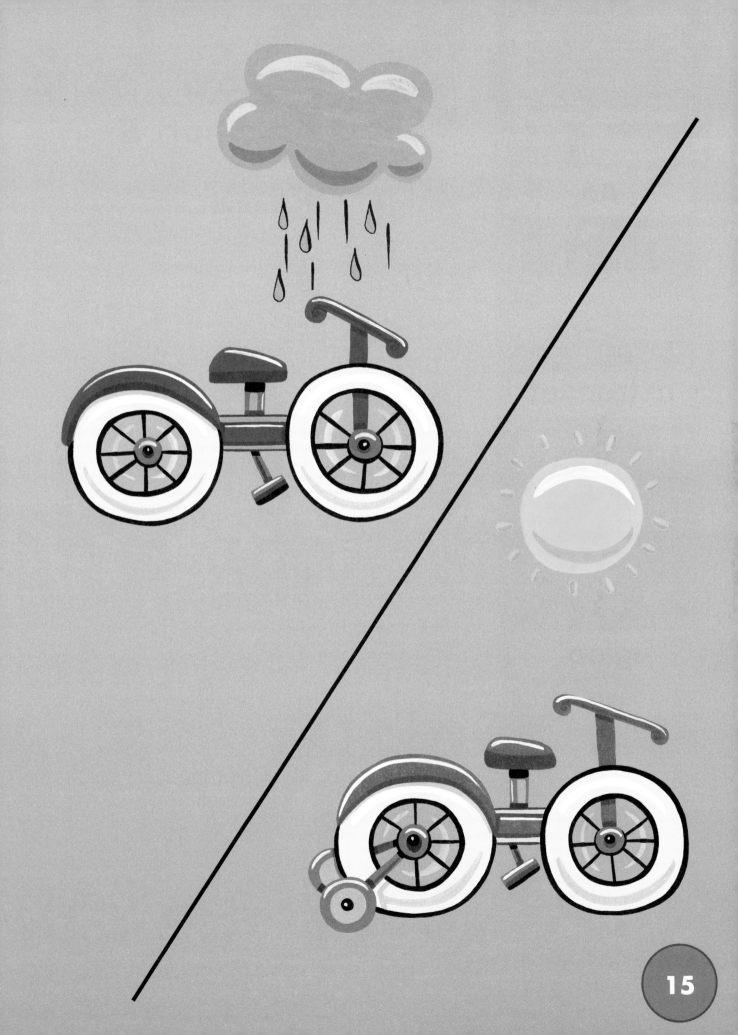

**Common Core State Standards**
**Foundational Skills 3.b.** Associate the long and short sounds with the common spellings (graphemes) for the five major vowels. **Also Foundational Skills 3.c.**

## Envision It! | Sounds to Know

### Aa

**astronaut**

### Ii

**igloo**

**READING STREET ONLINE**
**ALPHABET CARDS**
www.ReadingStreet.com

Phonics

# Short *Aa*, Short *Ii*

## Words I Can Blend

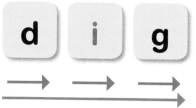

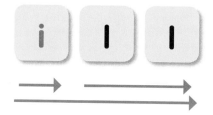

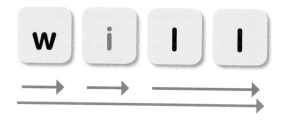

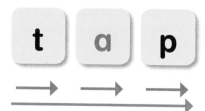

s  n  a  p

## Words I Can Read

here

do

little

with

what

## Sentences I Can Read

1. Here is the red bag.

2. Do you like it?

3. Yes, a little red bag is fun.

4. It will go with us on the bus.

5. What is in the bag?

**Common Core State Standards**
**Foundational Skills 4.** Read emergent-reader texts with purpose and understanding.
**Also Foundational Skills 3.b., 3.c.**

# I Can Read!

## Decodable Reader

- Short *Aa*

| Sam | can | tap |
|-----|-----|-----|
| Cat | pass | gap |
| nap | | |

■ Short *Ii*

| Kip | big | will |
|-----|-----|------|
| if | dig | Pig |
| fit | in | |

▲ High-Frequency Words

| is | little |
|----|--------|
| go | with |
| here | the |
| do | what |

★ Read the story.

**READING STREET ONLINE**
**DECODABLE eREADERS**
www.ReadingStreet.com

# If Kip Can

Written by Sara Blumenthal
Illustrated by Ken Ye

**Decodable Reader 31**

Kip is big.
Sam is little.
Sam will go with Kip.

If Kip can dig here,
Sam can dig here.
Kip can dig. Will Sam dig?

If Kip can tap Cat,
Sam can tap Cat.
Kip can tap Cat. Will Sam tap?

If Kip can pass Pig,
Sam can pass Pig.
Kip can pass Pig. Will Sam pass?

If Kip can fit in the gap,
Sam can fit in the gap.
Kip can fit. Will Sam fit?

If Kip can nap,
Sam can nap.
Kip can nap. Will Sam nap?

Sam can do what Kip can do!

# Envision It! Retell

**Big Book**

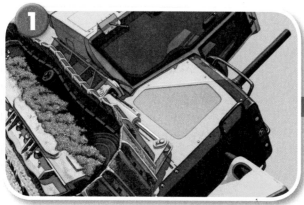

# Think, Talk, and Write

1. Think about *Dig Dig Digging.* How is *Building with Dad* like *Dig Dig Digging?*

**Text to Text**

2. How are a steamroller and a cement mixer alike? How are they different?

**Compare and Contrast**

3. Look back and write.

## Let's Learn It!

### Vocabulary

- Talk about the pictures.
- ■ Make compound words with words you know.

### Listening and Speaking

- Say a line from a nursery rhyme with a group.

Vocabulary

# Compound Words

 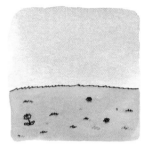

play **+** ground **=**

playground

book **+** shelf **=** bookshelf

class **+** room **=** classroom

# Recite Language

Be a good speaker!

Common Core State Standards
**Informational Text 1.** With prompting and support, ask and answer questions about key details in a text. **Also Informational Text 2.**

# Two Kinds of Homes

## Let's Practice It!

### Expository Text

- What will this selection be about? How do you know?

- Listen to the selection.

- What does the author tell about first? Second? Why does she do that?

- How are pueblos and tipis the same? How are they different?

- What questions do you have about these homes?

Some Native Americans built pueblos.

30

# Some Native Americans built tipis.

Common Core State Standards

**Foundational Skills 2.d.** Isolate and pronounce the initial, medial vowel, and final sounds (phonemes) in three-phoneme (consonant-vowel-consonant, or CVC) words.

# Let's Listen for

## Vowel Sounds

**Read Together**

- Point to the ox. Say the word. Say the beginning sound.

- Point to the top. Say the word. Say the middle sound.

- Find three things that begin with /o/, like *ox*. Find three things that have /o/ in the middle, like *top*.

- Point to these pictures and say the words: *ox, octopus, otter*. Do they begin the same? What about *cow, operation, fox?*

- Point to the top. What sounds do you hear in *top*? Separate the sounds with me: /t/ /o/ /p/.

**READING STREET ONLINE**
**BIG QUESTION VIDEO**
**www.ReadingStreet.com**

Comprehension

## Envision It!

### Literary Elements

**READING STREET ONLINE**
**ENVISION IT! ANIMATIONS**
www.ReadingStreet.com

## Characters

## Setting

34

## Plot

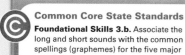
## Envision It! Sounds to Know

### Oo

### otter

**READING STREET ONLINE**
**ALPHABET CARDS**
www.ReadingStreet.com

Phonics

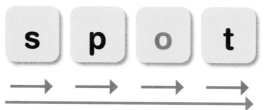 # Short o

## Words I Can Blend

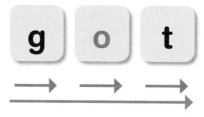

s p o t

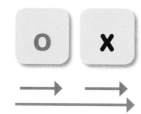

g o t

o x

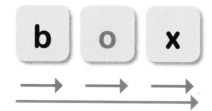

b o x

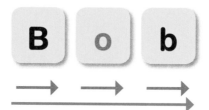

B o b

## Words I Can Read

| where |
|:---:|

| is |
|:---:|

| go |
|:---:|

| that |
|:---:|

| come |
|:---:|

## Sentences I Can Read

1. Where are Mom and Bud?

2. Mom is in the tent.

3. Bud did not go with Mom.

4. Bud is at that spot with Dad.

5. They will come in at six.

Common Core State Standards
**Foundational Skills 3.b.** Associate the long and short sounds with the common spellings (graphemes) for the five major vowels. **Also Foundational Skills 3.c., 4.**

Phonics

# I Can Read!

## Decodable Reader

- **Short Aa**
  | | | |
  |---|---|---|
  | Ann | Cass | sad |
  | ham | pan | pass |
  | can | yam | jam |
  | tan | | |

- **Short Ii**
  | | | |
  |---|---|---|
  | sit | Kim | did |
  | will | miss | it |
  | big | in | fix |
  | mix | dip | fill |
  | grin | sit | |

- **Short Oo**
  | | | |
  |---|---|---|
  | Tom | Jon | got |
  | not | hot | pot |

- **High-Frequency Words**
  | | |
  |---|---|
  | where | go |
  | is | a |
  | the | that |
  | with | |

- Read the story.

# Will Cass Come?

Written by Tracy Hawks
Illustrated by Bill Pars

Decodable Reader 32

Sit, Tom. Sit, Kim.
Sit, Ann. Sit, Jon.

Where did Cass go?
Cass will miss it.
Cass is sad.

Tom got a big ham.
Ham is in a big pan.
Pass us ham, Tom.

Ann can fix a yam.
It is not hot.
Pass us the yam, Ann.

Jon can mix dip.
Dip will fill that pan.
Pass us dip, Jon.

Kim can come with red jam.

Jam is in a tan pot.

Pass us red jam, Kim.

It is Cass!

Cass can grin.

Cass can sit with us.

**Common Core State Standards**
**Literature 1.** With prompting and support, ask and answer questions about key details in a text. **Also Literature 2., 3.**

**Trade Book**

# Envision It! | Retell

**READING STREET ONLINE**
**STORY SORT**
www.ReadingStreet.com

# Think, Talk, and Write

1. Which tools have you seen someone use? **Text to Self**

2. Which is a character from *Old MacDonald had a Woodshop*? What does she do in the story? **Character**

3. Look back and write.

**Common Core State Standards**
**Language 6.** Use words and phrases acquired through conversations, reading and being read to, and responding to texts. **Also Speaking/Listening 1.a.**

# Let's Learn It!

## Vocabulary

- Talk about the pictures.
- Where do you go if you want to ride a train?
- ▲ Where do firefighters work? Police officers?
- ★ Where do you go if you need gas for your car?

## Listening and Speaking

- Put your thumb up when you hear a fact.
- Put your thumb down when you hear an opinion.

## Vocabulary

# Location Words

## train station

## police station

## fire station

## gas station

# Discuss Fact and Opinion

Be a good listener!

49

# Let's Practice It!

## Lullaby

● Listen to the lullaby.

■ Clap your hands to show the beats.

▲ What line is repeated four times?

★ To whom is the lullaby sung? Why?

♥ What does the lambs' fleece look and feel like?

# Sleep, Baby, Sleep

# Let's Listen for

## Vowel Sounds

● Point to an elf. Say *elf*. Say the beginning sound.

■ Point to the bed. Say *bed*. Say the middle sound.

▲ Find three things that begin with /e/, like *elf*. Find three things that have /e/ in the middle, like *bed*.

★ Point to these pictures and say the words: *elephant, net, elbow*. Do they begin the same? What about *elk, elevator, egg*?

♥ Point to the bed. What sounds do you hear in *bed*? Separate the sounds with me: /b/ /e/ /d/.

**READING STREET ONLINE**
**BIG QUESTION VIDEO**
**www.ReadingStreet.com**

**52**

**Common Core State Standards**

**Informational Text 2.** With prompting and support, identify the main topic and retell key details of a text.

# Envision It!

## Main Idea

**READING STREET ONLINE**
**ENVISION IT! ANIMATIONS**
www.ReadingStreet.com

School

**Envision It!** | **Sounds to Know**

## Ee

## escalator

Phonics

# 🔊 Short e

## Words I Can Blend

m  e  n

→  →  →

r  e  d

→  →  →

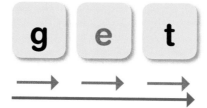

g  e  t

→  →  →

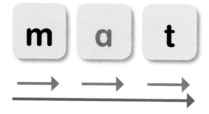

m  a  t

→  →  →

a  t

→  →

## Words I Can Read

| the |
| --- |

| was |
| --- |

| to |
| --- |

| like |
| --- |

| from |
| --- |

## Sentences I Can Read

1. The man had a big pet.
2. The pet was a tan dog.
3. The dog went to run.
4. Dogs like to run.
5. Dogs run from big cats.

Common Core State Standards
**Foundational Skills 3.b.** Associate the long and short sounds with the common spellings (graphemes) for the five major vowels. **Also Foundational Skills 3.c., 4.**

**Phonics**

# I Can Read!

## Decodable Reader

● Short *Aa*

| mat | sat | can |
|-----|-----|-----|
| pass | add | ham |
| and | | |

■ Short *Ee*

| Ed | red | hen |
|-----|-----|-----|
| egg | set | bed |
| well | net | |

▲ Short *Ii*

| big | in | it |
|-----|-----|-----|
| tin | Tim | grin |

★ Short *Oo*

| got | on | hop |
|-----|-----|-----|
| toss | pot | |

♥ High-Frequency Words

| a | the | what |
|-----|-----|-----|
| do | with | to |

◆ Read the story.

# The Red Egg

Written by Robert Smith
Illustrated by Perry Scott

**Decodable Reader 33**

Ed got a big,
red, hen egg.
Ed set the egg on a mat.

Ed sat on the bed.
What can Ed do
with the red egg?

Ed can hop well
with the red egg.
Hop, Ed, hop.

Ed can toss the red egg
in a big net.
Toss it, Ed.

Ed can pass the red egg
in a tin can.
Pass it, Ed.

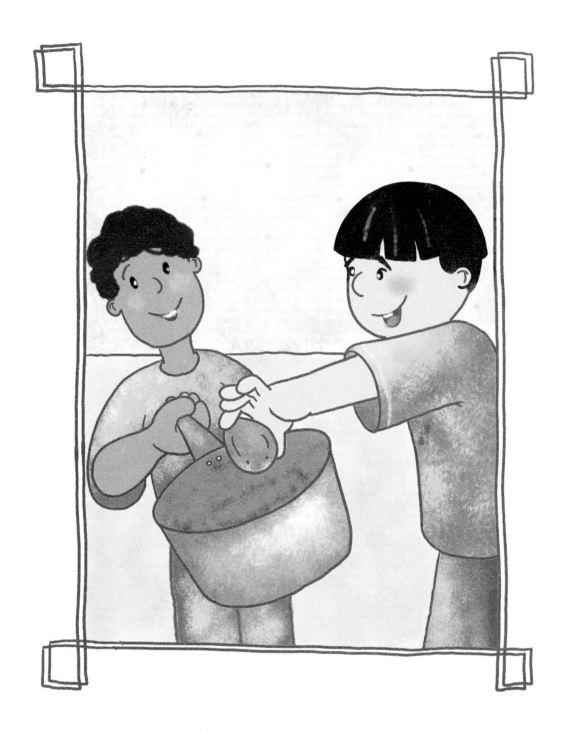

Ed can set the red egg
in a big pot.
Set it, Ed.

Ed can add ham
to the big, red, hen egg.
Ed and Tim can grin.

**Common Core State Standards**
**Informational Text 2.** With prompting and support, identify the main topic and retell key details of a text.
**Also Informational Text 1.**

**Big Book**

# Envision It! | Retell

**READING STREET ONLINE**
**STORY SORT**
www.ReadingStreet.com

**66**

# Think, Talk, and Write

**1.** What does a beaver use to cut down trees and build its house? Text to World

**2.** What is the story *Building Beavers* mostly about?

Main Idea

**3.** Look back and write.

# Let's

**It!**

## Vocabulary

● Talk about the pictures.

■ Which actions can you do?

## Listening and Speaking

● Point to Sign 1. What do you do when you see this sign?

■ Point to Sign 2. What does this sign mean?

▲ Point to Sign 3. What does this sign mean?

# Words for Actions

dig

carry

eat

sleep

**68**

# Interpret Information

1.

2.

3.

Be a good listener!

# The Milkmaid and Her Pail

## Let's Practice It!

### Fable

● Listen to the fable.

■ What happens to the pail of milk? What does this do to the milkmaid's plan to get a new dress?

▲ Tell in your own words what the moral means.

★ Why do people listen to or read fables?

70

71

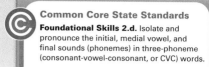

**Common Core State Standards**
**Foundational Skills 2.d.** Isolate and pronounce the initial, medial vowel, and final sounds (phonemes) in three-phoneme (consonant-vowel-consonant, or CVC) words.

**Phonemic Awareness**

# Let's Listen for

**Read Together**

## Vowel Sounds

- ● Point to the up arrow. Say *up*. Say the beginning sound.

- ■ Point to the sun. Say *sun*. Say the middle sound.

- ▲ Find three things that begin with /u/, like *up*. Find three things that have /u/ in the middle, like *sun*.

- ★ Say these words: *umbrella*, *up*, *ax*. Do they begin the same? What about *up*, *umpire*, *under*?

- ♥ Point to *up*. What sounds do you hear in *up*? Separate the sounds with me: /u/ /p/.

**READING STREET ONLINE**
**BIG QUESTION VIDEO**
www.ReadingStreet.com

73

**Common Core State Standards**
**Literature 3.** With prompting and support, identify characters, settings, and major events in a story.

**Comprehension**

# Envision It!

## Literary Elements

**READING STREET ONLINE**
**ENVISION IT! ANIMATIONS**
www.ReadingStreet.com

## Characters

## Setting

## Plot

**Envision It!** | **Sounds to Know**

## Uu

## umbrella

**READING STREET ONLINE**
**ALPHABET CARDS**
www.ReadingStreet.com

Phonics

# Short *u*

## Words I Can Blend

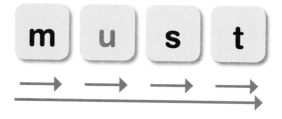

m  u  s  t

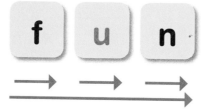

f  u  n

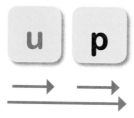

u  p

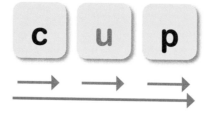

c  u  p

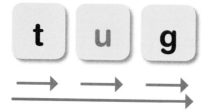

t  u  g

## Words I Can Read

| for |
| --- |

| my |
| --- |

| of |
| --- |

| we |
| --- |

| yellow |
| --- |

## Sentences I Can Read

1. That gift is for me.

2. My mom got it for me.

3. It is a big box of hats.

4. We like to dress up.

5. The yellow hat is best.

77

**Common Core State Standards**
**Foundational Skills 3.b.** Associate the long and short sounds with the common spellings (graphemes) for the five major vowels. **Also Foundational Skills 3.c., 4.**

**Phonics**

# I Can Read!

## Decodable Reader

- ● Short *Aa*
  | can | fast |
  |-----|------|
  | lap | had |

- ■ Short *Ee*
  pet

- ▲ Short *Ii*
  | big | will | hill |
  |-----|------|------|
  | dig | in | did |
  | sip | if | it |
  | sit | | |

- ★ Short *Oo*
  | Spot | not | lot |
  |------|-----|-----|
  | hot | on | top |

- ♥ Short *Uu*
  | pup | run | fun |
  |-----|-----|-----|
  | up | mud | tug |
  | hug | jump | |

- ◆ High-Frequency Words
  | is | my | a |
  |----|-----|------|
  | for | the | of |
  | I | with | what |
  | we | | |

- ❀ Read the story.

**READING STREET ONLINE**
**DECODABLE eREADERS**
www.ReadingStreet.com

# Fun with Spot

Written by Cassandra Belton
Illustrated by Joseph Green

**Decodable Reader 34**

Spot is my pup.
Spot is not a big pet.

Spot can run fast.
Spot will run for fun.
Spot will run up the hill.

Spot can dig.

Spot will dig in the mud.

Spot will dig up a lot of mud.

Spot can tug.
I will tug with Spot.
What did Spot tug?

Spot can sip.
If it is hot,
Spot will sip a lot.

Spot can sit.
Spot will sit on my lap
on top of the hill.

I will hug Spot.
Spot had fun.
We will jump up.

# Envision It! Retell

**Trade Book**

# Think, Talk, and Write

Read Together

1. How are Alistair and Kip like other friends we have read about? How are they different? **Text to Text**

2.

| Beginning | |
|-----------|--|
| Middle | |
| End | |

Choose an important part of the story. Act it out with some friends. ⟳ Plot

3. Look back and write.

# Let's Learn It!

## Vocabulary

- Talk about the pictures.
- ■ Where can you go if you are hurt?
- ▲ Where can you go if you need food? Money?
- ★ Where can you go to wash your clothes?

## Listening and Speaking

- What do we learn about Max and Uncle Bunny in the story?
- ■ What do we learn about Ruby in the story?
- ▲ What events in the story show what Max, Uncle Bunny, and Ruby are like?

Vocabulary

# Location Words

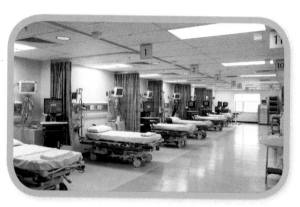
hospital

bank

grocery store

laundromat

# Discuss Literary Elements
## Character

Be a good listener!

# Going to the Library

# Let's Practice It!

## Signs

● Listen to the selection.

■ What is the selection about?

▲ Point to each sign. Tell what it means.

★ What do you notice about the shapes and colors of the signs?

♥ Why are traffic signs important?

✱ What questions do you have about these signs?

**Common Core State Standards**
**Foundational Skills 2.** Demonstrate understanding of spoken words, syllables, and sounds (phonemes).
**Also Foundational Skills 2.a., 2.d.**

# Let's Listen for

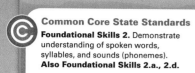

**Read Together**

## Consonant and Vowel Sounds

- Point to the bat. Say the word. Say the beginning sound. Find two more things that begin with /b/.

- Point to a cat. Say *cat*. Say the middle sound. Find two more things with /a/ in the middle.

- Blend /s/ /u/ /n/. What's the word? Yes, *sun*. Point to the picture.

- What is the last sound in *sun*? Point to two more things that end with /n/, like *sun*.

- Say *mug*. Name two things that rhyme with *mug*.

**READING STREET ONLINE**
**BIG QUESTION VIDEO**
www.ReadingStreet.com

92

93

**Comprehension**

# Envision It!

## Literary Elements

**READING STREET ONLINE
ENVISION IT! ANIMATIONS**
www.ReadingStreet.com

## Characters

## Setting

## Plot

Common Core State Standards
**Foundational Skills 3.** Know and apply grade-level phonics and word analysis skills in decoding words.
**Also Foundational Skills 3.a., 3.c.**

## Envision It! | Sounds to Know

### Dd

### dolphin

Phonics

# Decode Words

## Words I Can Blend

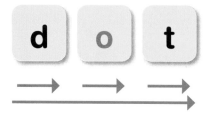

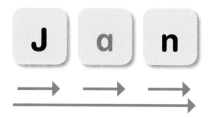

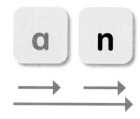

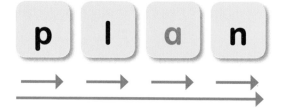

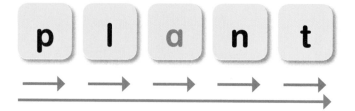

## Words I Can Read

| have |

| they |

| two |

| four |

| blue |

## Sentences I Can Read

1. We have a little plan.

2. They have a big plan.

3. We will get two to help.

4. They will get four.

5. Can we fill blue cups?

Common Core State Standards
**Foundational Skills 3.b.** Associate the long and short sounds with the common spellings (graphemes) for the five major vowels. **Also Foundational Skills 3.c., 4.**

**Phonics**

# I Can Read!

## Decodable Reader

- Short *Aa*

| | | |
|---|---|---|
| Jan | tan | had |
| fat | an | bat |
| can | | |

- Short *Ee*

| | | |
|---|---|---|
| red | net | wet |
| Deb | fed | Wes |
| hen | fell | egg |
| well | | |

- Short *Ii*

| | | |
|---|---|---|
| will | in | big |
| pig | Kim | slim |
| mitt | win | did |
| quit | | |

- Short *Oo*

| | | |
|---|---|---|
| Todd | got | hot |
| Rob | not | |

- Short *Uu*

| | | |
|---|---|---|
| fun | sun | mud |
| snug | run | |

- High-Frequency Words

| | |
|---|---|
| a | they |
| have | the |

- Read the story.

**READING STREET ONLINE
DECODABLE eREADERS**
www.ReadingStreet.com

# Fun in the Sun

Written by Harry Reynolds
Illustrated by Dan Vick

**Decodable Reader 35**

Todd got a red net.
Jan got a tan net.
Will they have fun?

Todd got wet.
Jan got wet.
They had fun in the hot sun!

Deb fed a big, fat pig.
Wes fed a red hen.
Will they have fun?

Deb fell in the mud.
Wes got an egg.
They had fun in the hot sun!

Kim got a slim bat.
Rob got a snug mitt.
Will they win?

Kim can run well. Kim did win.
Rob did not quit. Rob did win.

They had fun in the hot sun!

**Common Core State Standards**
**Informational Text 1.** With prompting and support, ask and answer questions about key details in a text.
**Also Informational Text 2., 3.**

# Envision It! Retell

**Big Book**

# Think, Talk, and Write

**1.** How does each one help build a house? *Text to World*

**2.** Where does the story *The House That Tony Lives In* take place? *Setting*

**3.** Look back and write.

## Vocabulary

- ● Talk about the pictures.
- ■ Show you are frightened.
- ▲ When might you feel worried?
- ★ When might you feel proud?
- ♥ Show you are angry.

## Listening and Speaking

- ● What is the title of the book?
- ■ Who is the author? Who is the illustrator?
- ▲ What is the setting of the story?
- ★ Tell what happens at the beginning, in the middle, and at the end of the story.

Vocabulary

# Words for Feelings

frightened

worried

proud

angry

# Oral Presentation
# Book Report

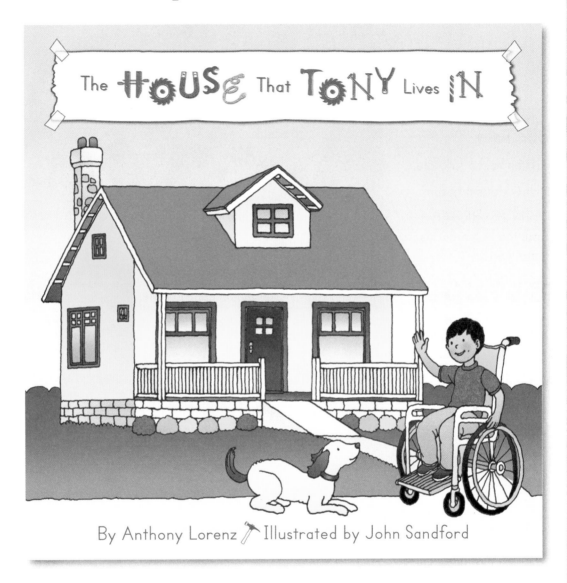

The HOUSE That TONY Lives IN

By Anthony Lorenz · Illustrated by John Sandford

Be a good speaker!

**Common Core State Standards**
**Literature 1.** With prompting and support, ask and answer questions about key details in a text. **Also Literature 2., 5.**

# Juan Bobo

## Let's Practice It!

### Folk Tale

● Listen to the folk tale.

■ How does it begin?

▲ Why does Juan Bobo put the burro on his shoulder?

★ Juan Bobo is a character in many Hispanic folk tales. Why do you think this is so?

♥ What can you learn from Juan Bobo?

**1**

**2**

111

# Let's Listen for

**Read Together**

## Blends

● Point to the broom. Say the word. Say the beginning blend. Find two more things that begin with /br/.

■ Point to the limb. Say *limb*. Say the middle sound. Find two more things with /i/ in the middle.

▲ Point to a plant. Say the word. Say the blend you hear at the end. Find two more things that end with /nt/.

★ Point to these pictures and say the words: *brown, bricks, brush.* Do they begin the same? What about *drink, sticks, broom?*

**READING STREET ONLINE**
**BIG QUESTION VIDEO**
www.ReadingStreet.com

**Common Core State Standards**
**Informational Text 1.** With prompting and support, ask and answer questions about key details in a text. **Also Informational Text 10.**

# Envision It!

## Draw Conclusions

**READING STREET ONLINE**
**ENVISION IT! ANIMATIONS**
www.ReadingStreet.com

# Happy Happy Happy Happy

**Envision It!** | **Sounds to Know**

## Yy

## yo-yo

## Ss

## salamander

**READING STREET ONLINE**
**ALPHABET CARDS**
www.ReadingStreet.com

Phonics

# 🎯 Decode Words

## Words I Can Blend

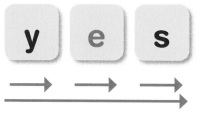

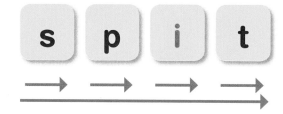

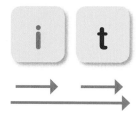

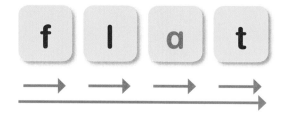

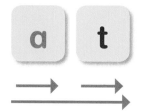

## Words I Can Read

you

see

said

look

three

## Sentences I Can Read

1. Do you see that?

2. "They are fast," said Dad.

3. "Look at the pups!" I said.

4. "I see three," Dad said.

5. Can I have a pup, Dad?

**Common Core State Standards**
**Foundational Skills 3.b.** Associate the long and short sounds with the common spellings (graphemes) for the five major vowels. **Also Foundational Skills 3.**

**Phonics**

# I Can Read!

## Decodable Reader

- ● Short *Aa*

| an | Pam | Cat |
|------|------|-----|
| can | had | tan |
| fan | flat | pan |
| ham | bad | |

- ■ Short *Ee*

| yes | let | bed |
|-----|-----|-----|
| red | fed | |

- ▲ Short *Ii*

| big | did | in |
|-----|-----|----|
| it | sit | |

- ★ Short *Oo*

| odd | box | Tom |
|-----|-----|-----|
| Fox | on | hot |
| not | | |

- ♥ Short *Uu*

| jump | yum | fun |
|------|-----|-----|

- ◆ High-Frequency Words

| what | said | I |
|------|------|------|
| see | you | the |
| a | with | they |
| for | | |

- ✱ Read the story.

# The Box

Written by Andrea Brooks
Illustrated by Linda Bird

Decodable Reader 36

"What an odd, big box!"
Pam Cat said.
"Can I see?"

119

"Yes, you can," said Tom Fox.
Tom Fox did let Pam Cat
see in the box.

Tom Fox had a tan bed
in the big box.
Tom Fox can jump on it.

Tom Fox had a red fan
in the big box.
Tom Fox can sit with the fan on.

Tom Fox had a flat pan
in the big box.
Tom Fox fed Pam Cat hot ham.

Pam Cat had hot ham
with Tom Fox.
Yum, yum! They had fun.

"Not bad for
an odd, big box,"
Pam Cat said.

# Envision It! | Retell

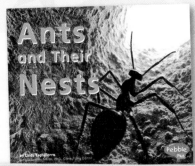

**Trade Book**

## Think, Talk, and Write

1. How are beavers and the way they build their homes like ants and the way they build their nests? **Text to Text**

2. Think about what **sticky** means. Why do you think ants use sticky silk to build their nests? **Draw Conclusions**

3. Look back and write.

**Common Core State Standards**
**Literature 3.** With prompting and support, identify characters, settings, and major events in a story. **Also Language 6.**

# Let's Learn It!

## Vocabulary

- Talk about the pictures.
- Which bugs have wings?
- ▲ Which bugs have you seen?

## Listening and Speaking

- Where does the story take place?
- During what season does the story take place?
- ▲ Why doesn't the story take place in the desert?

# Words for Bugs

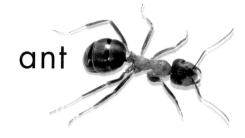

ant

bee

fly

spider

# Discuss Literary Elements
## Setting

Be a good listener!

**Common Core State Standards**
**Literature 5.** Recognize common types of texts (e.g., storybooks, poems).
**Also Foundational Skills 2.a.**

# A Man at a Restaurant in Crewe

## Let's Practice It!

### Poem

● Listen to the poem.

■ Clap your hands to show the beats.

▲ Which words rhyme?

★ Do you think the poem is funny? Why or why not?

♥ Why do people like to listen to or read this kind of poem?

# Words for Things That Go

airplane

bike

truck

car

bus

van

boat

train

# Words for Colors

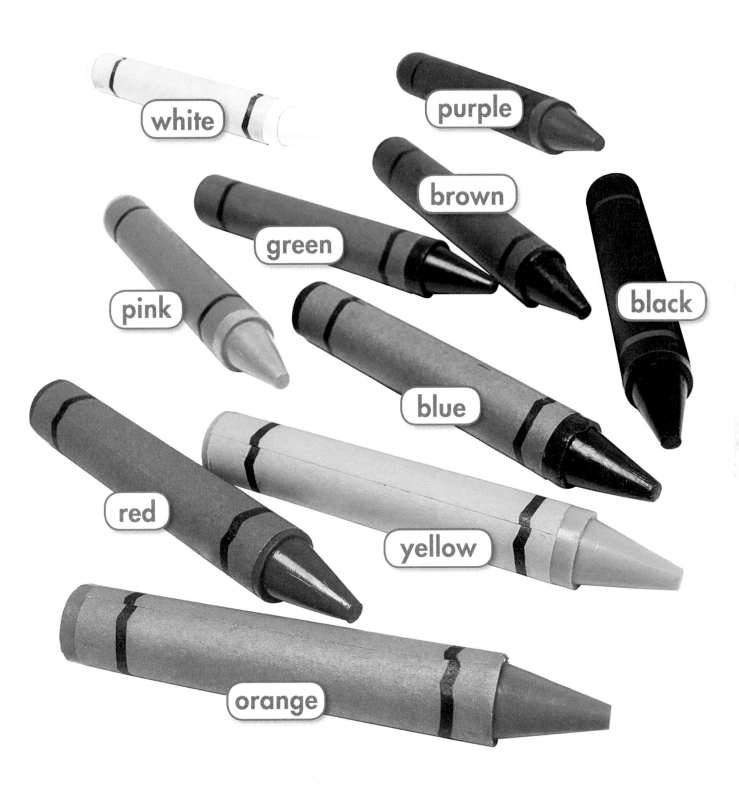

white

purple

brown

green

black

pink

blue

red

yellow

orange

# Words for Shapes

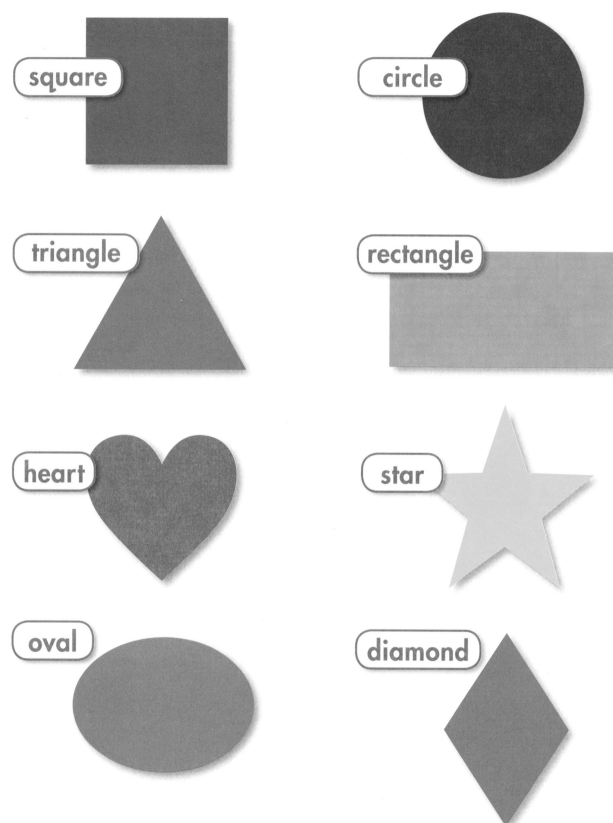

square

circle

triangle

rectangle

heart

star

oval

diamond

**134**

# Words for Places

school
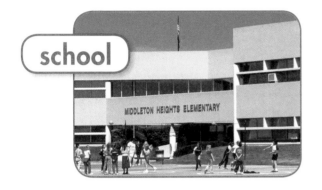

home

park

train station

police station

fire station

post office

library

# Words for Animals

lion

mouse

puppy

dog

cat

duck

turtle

kitten

chick

hen

rooster

bird

136

butterfly

fish

whale

caterpillar

bear

panda

beaver

calf

cow

# Words for Actions

skip

walk

run

fly

swim

ride

jump

hop

# Position Words

up

down

in

out

on

around

over

under

# My Classroom

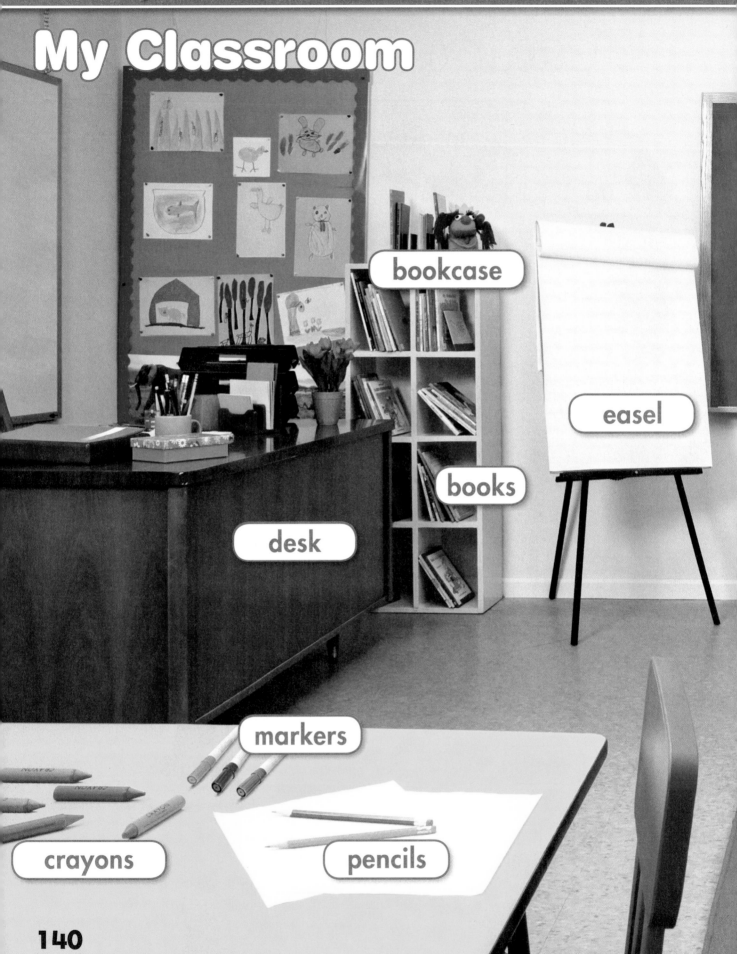

bookcase

easel

books

desk

markers

crayons

pencils

teacher

toys

paper

chair

blocks

table

rug

# Words for Feelings

happy

frightened

worried

excited

angry

proud

sad

surprised

# My Family

mom
mother

dad
father

sister

grandmother

brother

grandfather

# Acknowledgments

## Illustrations

**Cover:** Rob Hefferan

**12** Amanda Haley

**28–29, 49, 68, 108, 112** Anthony Lewis

**32** Jannie Ho

**39–45** Natalia Vasquez

**50** Karen Stormer Brooks

**52** Ron Lieser

**59–65** Maria Mola

**70–71** Martha Aviles

**72** Stephen Lewis

**79–85** Cale Atkinson

**90** Ivanke & Lola

**92** Jamie Smith

**99–105** Dani Jones

**110–111** Constanza Basaluzzo

**119–125** Robbie Short

**130–131** Cecilia Rebora

## Photographs

Every effort has been made to secure permission and provide appropriate credit for photographic material. The publisher deeply regrets any omission and pledges to correct errors called to its attention in subsequent editions.

Unless otherwise acknowledged, all photographs are the property of Pearson Education, Inc.

Photo locators denoted as follows: Top (T), Center (C), Bottom (B), Left (L), Right (R), Background (Bkgd)

**10** ©Harry Engels/Photo Researchers, Inc., (B) ©Ralf Gerard/Getty Images

**16** ©Jeri Gleiter/Getty Images, GRIN/NASA

**30** (T) ©Digital Focus/Alamy

**31** (T) ©Royalty-Free/Canada

**36** ©Dave King/DK Images

**48** ©David R. Frazier Photolibrary, Inc./Alamy Images, ©Enigma/Alamy Images, ©Visions of America, LLC/Alamy Images

**56** ©Dennis MacDonald/PhotoEdit

**88** ©David Young-Wolf/PhotoEdit Inc., ©Jeff Greenberg/Alamy Images, (T) ©Stock Connection Blue/Alamy Images, ©Tim Mantoani/Masterfile Corporation, Blend Images/Jupiter Images

**96** ©Stuart Westmoreland/Getty Images

**116** ©Zig Leszczynski/Animals Animals/Earth Scenes

**128** Frank Greenaway/©DK Images, Geoff Brightling/©DK Images, Tim Ridley/©DK Images

**132** (CR) ©Basement Stock/Alamy, (TR, TL, TC, BL) Getty Images

**133** (B) Getty Images

**136** (BR) ©Arthur Morris/Corbis, (CC) © Cyril Laubscher/DK Images, (TL) Dave King/DK Images, (BC) ©Gordon Clayton/DK Images, (CR) ©Karl Shone/DK Images, (CL) ©Marc Henrie/DK Images, (TR) DK Images, (TC, BCL) Getty Images, (BL) Jane Burton/©DK Images

**137** (CR) ©A. Ramey/PhotoEdit, ©Comstock Images/Jupiter Images, (CL) ©Cyndy Black/Robert Harding World Imagery, (CC) ©Dave King/DK Images, (BR, BC) ©Gordon Clayton/DK Images, ©Rudi Von Briel/PhotoEdit, (TC, BL) Getty Images

**138** (TR) Rubberball Productions, (BR) Jupiter Images, (TL) Photodisc/Thinkstock/Getty Images, (BC) Photos to Go/Photolibrary, (TC) Steve Shott/©DK Images

**139** (TR, TC) ©Max Oppenheim/Getty Images, (CR, BR) Getty Images, (C, BL) Rubberball Productions

**142** (CR) ©Ellen B. Senisi, (BL) ©Simon Marcus/Corbis, (TR/TL) Getty Images, (TC) Jupiter Images, (C) Photos to Go/Photolibrary, (BR) Rubberball Productions